The Cricket Song
Sounds of a Waking Poet

Nancy

Life is a Song
Sing Along!

Joan M Scharff

The Cricket Song
Sounds of a Waking Poet
Joan M. Scharff

The Cricket Song

Sounds of a Waking Poet

Cover Photography by
Catherine Scharff and Joan Scharff
Cover Design by Florence Schiavo
Photo of Goose by Jacqueline Karl Ferrell

This book is dedicated
to anyone seeking
their own sound;
to my son Michael
for his amazing presence and inspiration;
and to all teachers and guides -
past, present, and future
with my deepest
love and gratitude.

Table of Contents

The Magic of Life

Have you ever wondered where you belong?
Who will receive your next smile, hear your laughter, share your tears?
Who will understand things just the way you do?
Who knows you, who loves you?
On what foundation do you stand?
One day you realize you've opened so many doors, perhaps all the wrong doors.
Searching and looking for someone to notice who you are, even tell you who you are
Waiting and waiting for your moment, sure that this isn't the one
Afraid to take a step, afraid to miss it too
Have you been waiting for a hand to hold while you walk into the unknown?
Someone to show you the way and make it easy to cross the bridge
Looking in every pair of eyes, maybe these will be the eyes that see me
Maybe this one will help me become who I know I can be
But each pair asks for something
And it's easy to forget what you were looking for in the first place
Have you ever felt so young, so helpless, so scared, and have you been lost and unsure?
Waiting for someone to let you know that you are special, that you do have worth?
When you feel like there is no one to talk to or to understand
A moment comes along when you hear the cricket song and the sound reaches the heavens
And you ask, what is my song? What sound can I make?
What is the magic cricket sound I bring to the world?
Don't you have a sound to make?
Everything may have told you, it's not enough
You're not enough, or you're not ready. Everything may have told you to stay silent
Life may have convinced you that you're a bad seed, or worthless.
Then, as easily as you asked, you realize you are part of an entire symphony

And only you can sing your particular note
One day you realize, the eyes you've been waiting for are your own
The sound you make, is the only sound you can make
You look in the mirror, and wisdom looks back at you and smiles
And there as you cry your tears over never knowing, you may hear the simple answer
And you think, this can't be it, it's just too easy
Do what I love; do what I love; do what I love
With my whole heart
Sing my song, even if it's off key and nobody hears it
Make my sound, even if no one likes it
A funny thing happens when you start to sing
All eyes turn and look if only for a moment
And in that moment, you see the magic of love and recognition in every knowing pair
And it's as if every pair of eyes are your own eyes sparkling and shining back at you
And you know you are home
You accept that you are part of an amazingly imperfect world
Part of the magic of life

The Cricket Song

Each one has a sound
A solitary sound
Different, and unique
A sound that only they can make
Personal music
Yet when played naturally and freely
Unites as one great song
Expanding waves reaching to the Heavens
Touching the Moon
Circling the stars and returning like magic
To the peaceful and open heart

Photograph by Joan Scharff

Compassion

Early 20's

With understanding eyes I watch as life unveils her truths
Alone I stand and feel for her
Yet there is nothing I can do
What used to be a steady flame
Is now a raging fire
Its force burns not my pain away
Only my desire

Early 50's

With understanding eyes I watch as life unveils her truths
Some harsh and difficult
Some sweet and tender
Each moment an invitation
To allow deep roots
To spread and strengthen
Even In the harshest winter
Fire burns steady
Acceptance and peace settle in

Tiny Surgeon

Tiny hands of one so small
Holding ill and heavy, hardened heart
Larger than your own hands
Larger than your own heart
Hands so small and young, yet the only hands capable
To find the hidden treasure, joy

Lost in a stone of coal
Blackened and hard, edges greyed when fire went deep
Buried and locked away
Hidden from all
Like a tiny bird, without a sound
Tired of calling and waiting for its mother
Who never comes

Treasure only you can find
Small, tiny hands of Grace
Bring birds to peck open and cry screeching sounds
The heart's screams and calls of wanting, released
Ignite fury for not being heard, raging fire burn
Your tiny hands all the while weaving and mending

Hands transformed with ageless wisdom have surgeon's skill
Feet growing roots into the earth
Sparks with smiles fly out of finger branches
Preparing wings with loving touch
Pure and simple innocence
All of the tears, the drowning tears, now crystals sparkling
in the sun
Heart opens, out she flies

On wings of Grace soar treasured skies
Breathe spirit in and rest my child
Receive seeds of wisdom and grow as one
Hand and heart warmed by the sun
Prisms of colors shine in your eyes
Joy of living, a wonder surprise

Gathering Branches

Roots fractured by early death
Broken hearted, love lost
Scattered branches disappear
Spirits roam longing paths
Separate limbs that turn and twist
Vision clouded source unknown
Voices whisper barely heard
Haunted seekers journey far
Goose flies for miles and miles
Feathering Home to cleansing fire
Flames lick, clear branches of mire
Illuminate opening, map appear
Healing tears glisten in light
Walk through lifetimes of souls unknown
Gathering branches, twigs and bones
Calling the names, beckoning back
Invisible circuits start and snap
Evaporate fears, souls reunite
Wisdom of ages, your presence near
Love warming hearts, smiles burning bright
All invited to dance in the fire
Appreciate gifts and spirit flight

Photograph by Jacqueline Karl

Wise Sage

Goose meets eyes of an eagle
Whispers on wind
Spread your wings widely
So I may see you my friend

Hollow Chambers

Empty hollow heart lying alone
Sorrow to depth; overcome with despair
Sounds of birds, so many songs
Hidden from eye, your presence known
Swells hollow chambers and calms to the bone
Peace for a moment, surrender to songs
Wind rustles leaves
Gently fly near
Land so lightly
For a moment, home

Heavy Rain

Heavy rain, darkened room
Wind whipping and clashing with everything
Wanting to blow me off course
Nearly did
Worrying for the campers
Wanting to do or be something more
Frightened child
Why am I warm?
Hide my aching heart under warm blankets
I dare not say
Lay here, hide here
Warm cocoon
Wanting to give up, give in, give way
Listen to someone cry "I'll never be, I'll never have"
Notice shadows of mirror reflection
Waiting for something or someone to change them
Still and quiet in the darkened room
Hopelessness and helplessness pervasive
Alone under weight of heavy blankets
Cracked and broken child
Wanting to lay down and die
Contemplate what can I really do to help another?
In that moment, hear the song of a blackbird
A singing voice behind the wall, soothes
Are these songs not enough to lift?
Lift and move my helpless body
Feet on the floor
Take one step, just one toward the sound
Focus on the sun
Words on paper, fall heavy

Wind dies down
Rain lighter and softer
Eyes open
Join the sound of a lovely voice singing again in the distance
Words on paper, a few more
Magical blackbird sings reward
Only a note or two
Words on paper, soothes
My own words lifting
I've chosen well,
Today I wear my smile, today I am here and thankful
Cleansed by heavy rain and healing awareness.

Photograph by Joan Scharff

Listening

Fears and fragments
What if's and why's
Let go, come back
Like clouds in the sky
Drift ever so slowly
Ease on by
Rest in my heart
A moment of sun
Speak to me softly
I know we are one

Photograph by Joan Scharff

Dogwood Moment

Sunrise over trees;
Pink Blossoms Bright
Face washed with cool breeze;
Blue Sky Dream
Dogwood Moment

Mandala Welcome

He threw water in my face
Branch dipped in holy water
Waved with such strength and disdain
Smacked my face with a stinging force, soaked
Not sprinkled with love and greeting the way I wanted
The way it was intended by ceremony to Bless and welcome
All as One to sacred space
Entrance to holy place
Where Mandala turns, consciousness shifts and magic happens

He threw water in my face
Hit me in a way that felt like an assault
Scorn and anger swelled in my heart strong like the force of his blow
In that moment I hated him with every cell of my body
I wanted to strike with equal or stronger force
Who do you think you are?
I wanted to look right in his eyes and scream
Look what you've done, look who you've injured
You bastard

I wanted to strike back at him
Then I remembered to ask
What else is possible?
In that moment, in that very instant that I asked
It was there
Wisdom always there
Choice is ours to be made
Shift to greater consciousness

He threw water in my face
Why wouldn't he?
Isn't this just the way I treat myself?
Don't I injure myself by my own actions and neglect?
Is he not a mirror for this?
He sees it in me I'm sure of this

Mirror reflection clear and bright
To love him, is to love me
To forgive him, is to forgive me
I recognized his need
I recognized his emptiness
I felt compassion and love for him in his unawareness
These are the thoughts I put my energy toward
A smile met my lips and I grew
I felt grateful for his gift and his wisdom
Consciousness shifted and magic happened
Mandala Welcome

Storm in a Teacup

Frightening wrath
Scramble and swirl
Hurt all on your path
Pull me in and toss all about
I know who you are, you cannot hide
Your madness covers a small one inside
Helpless and scared you cover it up
A teaspoon of sugar, some cream in the cup
Soothed for a while, but only a while
Boil and bubble, hot liquid splatter
Burning all near
Confuse and batter
Your power looks mighty
It works for a while
Pain anger driven
Small one stays hidden
Awful behavior
Stir shame and disgust
Drink from the cup, drink it you must
Drink stormy liquid
Out pour the tears
Drink from the cup
Face all the fears
The thing that you hide from
Not nearly so tough
Swig and be filled
Each taste makes you stronger
Who do you serve
Small one, no longer
Another big swig

A gulp of the poison
Power is greater than you could imagine
Soft, ever so sweet
Gift is uncovering
Storm in a Teacup
Gentle and loving

Here and Now

I Am Here Now
Look at Me
I am a woman standing up
No longer waiting for you to lift me, to show me, to give
me permission
I have the power to choose
I choose to stand up
Here and Now

I am standing up
No longer hiding because my ability, strength and
light scare you
No longer hiding from myself
I am unwilling to accept less because you undervalue me
I value me
The greatest gift I give and receive is to know who I am
and to meet you there, eye to eye
I have the wisdom to know that my strength
is your strength too
Stand with me

Don't let my gentle ways fool you
Soft, easy, perfume and flowers
Small things, feminine things have great power
I am larger and stronger than you might want to believe
I have endured, I know my strength

I care deeply
You see I will make a difference in this world

I have important things to say
My heart wants what is best for all
Stand beside me
You might be pleasantly surprised at what we know and can do together
This arsenal of difference might even enlighten

No Better, no worse, just different
Perhaps this world needs something different now
I wonder if I'm standing up right on time
Here and Now

I am the star who sparkles in the night sky
I am the eyes whose tears cleanse the earth and light the world with
loving kindness
I am the sun, whose warmth touches your face
I am the laughter that bubbles up, fills a room and opens your heart with
pure pleasure
I am your darkest moment of grief calling forth something new

I am the bird, whose melody invites joy and appreciation
I am the soft touch that comfort holds and reassures you
I am the strength that endures, giving without concern
for the cost
I am the vessel that brings life through it

I am the right words, at the right time, that invite you to grow
I am a tiny spark and a raging flame
I am a mountain whose power and majestic beauty inspire
I am small and humble enough to know that the power of faith and
forgiveness can crumble walls
and stop wars in an instant
Yes, I said this instant

I am a woman standing up
When I stand up I am fully aware
I am the clear blue sky aware of all that looks to it and flies through it

Every single drop in the ocean coming together as one great soothing
force
It seems to me that the world needs soothing now

When I stand up, I demand respect
I stand with respect for all around me, every small and natural thing is a
part of who I am
I am a force to be reckoned with
I invite you to stand with me
Meet me here, eye to eye
I hope you will
Here and Now

The Presence of Old (Ghost Squatters)

The past is gone, is it not?
What lingers?
Every present moment missed unless befriended old
Invisible lines holding on
Ancient power lines
Yesterday's strings reaching today
Steal the moments
Reach backward and forward
Today, tomorrow, ancient history

Strings unseen that have the power to move us
Hold us, pull us and bind us;
All the while choosing distraction, unawareness
Heartaches, betrayals, losses
Sometimes ours, sometimes those we love, sometimes ancient secrets
held
All here now

Heartaches we have caused and those imposed on us or on those we love
We hold them and carry them uninvited
Wounds; uninvited guests settled in to our muscles, bones and spaces
deep within us

Squatters

Strings that won't be denied, tied to yesterday, tangling present moment
Invisible power lines, yet strong as steel like prison bars solid enough to
keep criminals and innocent prisoners captive
Lines stopped and blocked by painful memories

Squatter wounds

Wounds we lick
Head in sand, dirt under carpet, try to deny their presence
They laugh and wait

There, within the bite, the swig, the stick, the distraction;
Wounds linger and lay waiting to take our hearts
Exhaled, like cigarette smoke, wounds fill a room and their stench
permeates our clothing and clouds our vision with despair
Wounds that can stop the flow and hold the pain of the past, and carry it
to the future
Unresolved wounds
Like seeds, lie dormant waiting for ideal conditions.
Unless faced, old wounds have the power to change today and hurt
tomorrow
Invisible strings

Wounded ghost squatters.

These strings connect us
Past, present, future
Grandfather, mother, sister, brother, master, boss, we are one
Lied to, liar
Raped, rapist
Battered, batterer
Neglected, neglector
Betrayed and betrayer
Abused or Abuser we are one
Strings of stories untold or hashed over and over
What strings pull and bind?
What invisible strings?
Some known, some forgotten, some remembered, some long ago secrets
untold
Ghost squatters holding on, waiting for their moment

What are they waiting for?
What do they want from us these squatters?
What gift and challenge do they bring us?

Wounded squatters waiting for invitation
Stand up, take my hand
Acknowledge, feel, honor
They are part of you; yesterday, today, tomorrow

You hold the power to know them
Flip the switch. Invite squatters to stand up
Truth illuminates and guides

Call to the past
Acknowledge their presence
Healing intention, invite and allow love to fill the spaces where even as
your heart breaks open, gripping anguish and despair are freed
Endure, bleeding moments of darkness, endure
Love heals all wounds
Squatters transform and take flight
Softening wisdom through muscles and bones, filling the spaces where
squatters once held
Sorrow slips away, peace moves in

Wall Street Petunias

Purple, pink happy faces
Lined up in precision rows
Like a marching band stand ready to perform
Bright colored petunia faces draw eyes in

Pink, Purple trumpets
Quiet musical presence
Petunias stand at attention;
Green life & vibrant color where dry brown dirt and scattered weeds
once were;

Flowers bloom pleasure for eyes and hearts
Gentle waves in wind salute
Civilian soldiers pass every working day to battle daily grind;
Breathe deeper in that moment

Do what must be done for families unaware
Enter clouded spaces; halls of smoke and mirrors
Minds confused with ethical lies
Feet tangled; snakes in grass

Petunias stand at attention
Planter's deception yet unknown
Purple, Pink petunia faces
Clarity arrives with Wall Street Generals

Petunias salute financial dignitaries
Minor detail in grand scheme perceived;
Clever value added, affordable
Strategically planted pomp and circumstance

Claw and clutch positions long held
Desperate to dazzle important visitors faltering faith
With politics and fate unknown;
Scramble and chaos flies under radar
Subtly steal character and integrity; slow leaking life force
Unintended lights dim; more for less
Less for more; more less
One grand day and show is over

Reap what you sow
It only takes time
Wall Street Petunias
Shrivel and die

Wall Street Petunias (another version)

One spring day we passed you by
Bright colored flowers where never before
Petunias planted for passing workers
Mark the end of long winter days, happy to leave them behind
Flowers bloom pleasure for eyes and heart
Fresh spring morning dew glistens and sparkles
Color and life fill barren space
Where grey brown dirt and scattered weeds once were
Pink, purple, green colors caught my eye
Breathe deeper in this moment
Your presence uplifting
A welcome addition, joy lingers

Petunias planted for Civilian soldiers
Who pass every working day to battle daily grind
Something to brighten our moments of duty
Something to notice while walking through fields of cracked black
asphalt and steel
All in a day's work, day after day
Enter clouded spaces to do what must be done
To provide for families unaware
Of the secrets held and the stories inside
Your simple floral presence a valued gift

Important visitors announced same day
Clarity arrives and clouds move in
Grand scheme perceived
Petunias stand at attention
To honor Wall Street Generals
Strategically planted pomp and circumstance
Clever value-added, affordable
Planter's deception revealed
Your perfect rows of bright colored trumpets
Planted and poised to dazzle financial dignitaries
Like marching band ready to perform
Petunias stand at attention
Everyday worker not part of the plan
Grey brown dirt and scattered weeds stir under radar
One grand day and show is over
Old roots take hold, ready to choke
Saddened hearts breathe shallow in this moment
Forgotten petunia
Desperate drought
Reap what you sow
It only takes time
Wall Street Petunias
Shrivel and die

Awakening

In Winter's Darkness, life lies still;
Sleepy, restful, waiting
To be kissed by the sun's warmth
To be nourished by the gentle rain
To dance freely in the wind
Spring's promise

The Sun's warmth growing stronger
Beckoning changes
Little by little emerging
Steadily calling forth
A new life and purpose
Awakens

Wisdom Whispers

Wisdom whispers in my ear
Here in this moment, stay here
Expansive Sky
Drifting clouds
You are near
The sounds, the scent,
The softness
The surety of this moment
Life singing, humming
Nature's music gently rocks and cradles
Soft drumming of my heart
Grows stronger with every grateful beat

Shadow Walk

I took a walk one day and came upon a wall
Of rocks so strong and wise
Majestic beauty, stand there for me
Protected and protector
Stones sparkle and reflect light
Cracks and crevices reveal something deeper
Water trickles out, glistening in the sun
The rock, the fortress
Amazed at your beauty and strength
At life rooting and springing out of the cracks
Just enough to give
I love every part of you

Fallen Heart

Forgiveness
As death of fallen tree
Returned to its beginning
Feeds the soil
Surrender,
Heart and soul;
Hard and brittle
Cracks and seeps its essence
Letting go of what it held
Decay and return
To soft earth
For new life will emerge
And one day bloom again

Heart Tree

Broken Heart
It is a privilege
To love and break so far in two
You've earned the life, and grown the wisdom
Your gift to others, their gift to you.

Eyes

It seems to me as I meet them
Pair after pair of eyes
The stories
So individual
So universal
Meet my heart

In Glastonbury, a pair vacant and haunting
Left me wondering about the harsh life
What took the presence from them?
Left in darkness with only a flash of piercing light
Seemed as if a fragment of soul remained
Enough to muddle through the long days

In Compton Dundon, eyes so knowing and loving
With presence inviting my own to slow and hold
The healing gaze
Of long ago wisdom
And love unattached
Strong and transforming

Eyes, so different, yet the same
Remembering those eyes familiar
Belonging to souls of my past loves
And of souls who no longer walk here with me
If I could look into them now
So different each pair I'd see

Something new and stronger
Yet old as eternity

Wild and free
Soft and loving
As light and joyful as newborn eyes
Full of thankfulness and acknowledgement for life

Meeting each pair of eyes
With honor and acceptance
Of the lifetimes that shaped them
Wanting to see them now again, touch them, and hold each gaze with
tenderness and love
So individual, so universal
Nothing different, only me

Waves

The horizon smiled today
A smile that sank deeply into my belly
The sunlit sky on fire with its warm colors
Orange, pink, crimson

Set waves of slowed breath
Rippling
Gently in and out, over and over
Like the tide
Transforming repetition

All that is there, clear and moving
Each breath deeper and freer than the last
Expansive, like the colors of the sky
Orange, pink, crimson smiles

Old resentments and fears washed away
Worn down with waves of breath
Shells tumbled in the ocean
Until only little fragments and chips remain
Swallowed by the sea
Taken to the greatest depth and loved there

What is, what was, what could never be
Simply smiled upon
The world changed with each breath
Orange, pink and crimson waves

The Little Things for Thanking

A cup of hot tea with pure raw honey and cream
Enough to warm on a dark and rainy day
Brings thoughts of the bees and the flowers

Warms to my toes
Rooted in the same earth
Of creation and buzzing flower essence

Life that made the sweet substance and the hands that harvested it
Hearing my son's laughter and witnessing his happiness
His smile so sweet, sweeter than any nectar, always brings a grateful
smile to my face

Gaze into his eyes, warmed deeply, pure raw honey for the heart
My dog batting me with her paw, and nibbling at my hand wanting to
play
Rolling over for the belly rub soon after

Her knowing eyes, the gift of fur and contentment and warmth to touch
Watch her receive love so easily and freely,
knowing I can too
A friend who finds humor in every day, who makes me laugh so hard
and fully

Really wishing someone well
Even someone who has hurt me deeply
So thankful for the wisdom to accept and forgive

A memory of a long ago story told by my mother
Reliving the moment and laughter in the telling, as if it were happening
to her right then
Tickles my nose and causes my eyes to water just in the remembering of
how she laughed

The broken moments, the ones that stung, like a slap in the face
Intended to stretch and pull me up
The hands and hearts that extended and helped to lift me

For this present moment
The sounds of life surrounding me, the ability to be here now
For all the little things...the little things for thanking

For the Birds (A Medley)

Sweet Song
Sweet song sung softly
As morning light ascends;
Grateful Presence
Messengers between worlds
Welcome visitors, they soothe the soul
Known sometimes by their chirps and chatter,
Flutters, squawks and noisy clatter
Winged friends of many colors
Even in silence, we know they are near

For All Who Listen
Love is like a bird in song
Sounds touch the world sweetly
Rejoice in their music
Sing for all who listen
One need simply listen

Calm and Sure
Eagles Nest
Calm and sure
Land and wait
Watchful eye
Eagle fly
Touch the sky
Silence speaks
Spirits Soar

Moth

Light of deception
Exhausting possibility
Fly toward it
Again and again
Unaware and misdirected
Caught in loop
Like a moth
Short-circuited, irregular
Seeking wrong source
Of light
Of acknowledgement

Change course now
Flight path recalculated
Into darkness unknown
Deeply listening
Faint direction at first
Source grows stronger
Within stillness find
A quiet place
Of illumination
Of clarity

Warrior Child

I want to meet every single hand and tongue
That dares to raise and threaten another
Meet it with its dark might
I want to grip its brutal force
That scares and intends to hurt
Someone kinder
I want to stop it fast in its tracks
With a mighty and fierce love
True power and grace
Wears any face
I want to show it itself
And like a great wild and forceful wind
Blow its deceptive authority and pain away
I want to scatter and change it
Leaving only tears behind
That when caught with my open hands and heart
Can witness its transformation
The warmth of the sun softening and clearing
Melting the harshness into recognizable relief
I want to meet and smile at
The gentle and healed spirit
That remains

Your Gift

Brought with purpose
Delivered
Not always to a grateful receiver
Now holds a place of great honor
Appreciation
For all the ways
You invite me to grow
Open heart allows
Eyes fill with sacred tears
Rolling with awareness of your immense power
Receiving your unspeakable love
Acknowledging
Your gift

Photograph by Joan Scharff

Words

Words
Have Presence
Lasting Presence
They linger for years, maybe even decades

Words
Awaken
In the night without even a sound
Wanting to move from deep sleep and warm covers through reluctant
hands to paper

Words
Have awareness and energy
They can inspire, dance and lift
They mix and mingle, like flavors in a great pot of soup

Words
Hot as hell, can burn and wound deeply
We ingest them and become them
We spill and roll them off our tongues, too easily and without care
sometimes

Words
Stay with us, fill gaps and spaces
They wedge themselves between us
Weaving fear and distrust with only the memory of them

Words
Can nourish and enlighten
And spoken softly, with love and kind intention
Have the greatest ability to heal and uplift

Words
Silent, unspoken and still
Hold great power, speak volumes
To those who listen

Sandy's Voice

She began in the sea
One elongated tropical wave
Humming along quietly
Her voice unnoticed at first
Gathering strength and momentum as she traveled

What to do?
Watch her come?
Sit and Wait
Avert our gaze, look away?
Business as usual?

Intensity grows in warm waters
Energy fueled at alarming rates
Amplified power
Sandy has something to say
Better listen
Atmosphere ripe for harvest
Nature's grief
Prepare to feel it

Her voice spans 1000 miles
Adversity makes landfall
"Super Storm" yields the unyielding
With an artist's fury
Brush strokes wild on canvas
Despair and devastation
She stretched over the land of 15 States
Wiping out landscapes with anguished strokes
Her voice singing out loud and clear
Screaming, gaining attention

Lives lost
Damages cost
Estimated $30 to $50 Billion
12,500 flights cancelled

Impact felt around the world

The world.

Economic and environmental loss
Far reaching
Wall Street stopped in its tracks
Election plans threatened
Mass transit halted
Millions lost power
Shorelines evacuated
Governor's orders
Inland residents advised to stay at home
She was "unprecedented"
"Frankenstorm delays Halloween"

Sandy has the voice of adversity
A great teacher
For great listeners
What is she saying?
Wisdom blows in with gale force winds
Gaining attention of those who would rather not hear
Yet the need to hear and heal is great
And the lessons need to be given
Atmosphere ripe for harvest
Always a blessing, always a blessing
Adversity is a great teacher
For those who will receive her

Straddle Fences

Lift yourself
Take your leg and remove it from the seemingly safe ground
Straddling fences is yesterday's news
Lift your leg from the place where those who say they love you stand
and approve
Why do you work so hard to fit here?
What is it that they know of who you are?
Authentic ground awaits arrival
Go
Move to the side where both feet are together
Stand true for once
Dare to see truth
They may not like you
Stand, regardless
Steady yourself
Not in righteousness, nor judgment
Alone, yet in strange company
Be true
Some familiar things will slip from your hands
Don't worry they were not yours to hold onto
Some you love may turn and walk
Leaving you standing alone
On shaky feet and steady ground
A puddle of disillusionment drying
As the clouds clear and sun touches
Notice the fullness and smile wide
Roots are strong here

Plugging In

What is it that I live and breathe each moment?
What choice do I have?
When racism rears its ugly face
With its violence, slurs and hate
Wanting to poke holes in my heart

When its rise is stoked and it can be felt in body and mind
What choice do I have?
Do I wear it like a heavy coat?
Or do I feel justified to stare it down and threaten it?
Do I run and hide?
What do I plug into?
What choice do I have?
Can I look away with love, breathe easy and accept what lies deep in the
eyes and heart of it?

When fear is palpable
And images of suffering fly fast and furious from talking boxes
When devastation is near enough to notice, feel and breathe
What lens will I look through?
What do I plug into?
What choice do I have?
If I choose worry and despair, what then do I really bring to help?
Do I breathe it in or can I exhale softly

Yes, these things exist
Hate, sadness, suffering
Helen said, "keep your face to the sunshine"
I think I will
Yes these things exist, and so do my choices
No not head in the sand

I know they are there
But I choose to see the human hand extend in love again and again
I choose the awareness that adversity brings a gift
Hardships are building blocks
I chose to see, yes I do, and I choose to look away from fear and anger
By doing so I hope to somehow lift
With my humble heart, and the deepest love and acceptance I am
capable of

Photograph by Joan Scharff

Ruthless

If I could gather a thousand smiles
And put them in your open hands
Or write a thousand poems
It wouldn't be enough to say what my heart feels
Gentle strength
Kind patience
Steady love
Willingness to listen and witness
Even to bitter deception
Navigated for truth's arrival
Your integrity
Leaves me breathless and deeply drenched in gratitude
With awe for the Divine

Snowy Night

A dark Winter's night
Clouds white as the snow that falls from them
Silence drops effortlessly
Like the snow, a soft layer
A blanket of stillness that covers all
A quiet, wondrous moment
No sound at all
Just gentle movement of cold white snow
Meeting eyes and face lightly
On a cold, dark night
Snowy path of silent peace

Made in the USA
Charleston, SC
24 February 2013